MY SiDEWALKS ON
SCOTT FORESMAN
READING STREET

Practice Book

Level
A

PEARSON

Scott
Foresman

Editorial Offices: Glenview, Illinois • Parsippany, New Jersey
New York, New York
Sales Offices: Boston, Massachusetts • Duluth, Georgia
Glenview, Illinois • Coppell, Texas • Sacramento, California • Mesa, Arizona

ISBN: 0-328-21382-9

12 13 14 15 V016 13 12 11 10 09

Contents

Name_____

Say the word for each picture.
Circle the picture if the word begins
with the **m** sound heard in **mat**.

_m_at

1.

2.

3.

4.

5.

6.

7.

8.

9.

10.

11.

12.

 Home Activity This page practices words that have the _m_ sound heard in _mail_. Work through the items with your child. Then walk through the house with your child and ask him or her to point out things that begin with the _m_ sound.

© Pearson Education A

Practice Book Unit 1

Phonics Mm/m/ **1**

Name_____

Say the word for each picture.
Circle the picture if the word begins
with the **t** sound heard in **table**.   <u>t</u>able

1.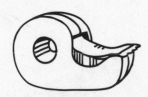

2.

3.

4.

5.

6.

7.

8.

9.

10.

11.

12.

School + Home

Home Activity This page practices words that have the *t* sound heard in *tag*. Work through the items with
your child. As you read with your child, encourage him or her to point out words that begin with the *t* sound.

2 Phonics Tt/t/   **Practice Book Unit 1**

Name_____

Say the word for each picture.
Write a on the line if you hear the
short **a** sound heard in **mat**.

m<u>a</u>t

1.

c _____ t

2.

f _____ sh

3.

p _____ n

4.

b _____ t

5.

s _____ n

6.

b _____ g

7.

l _____ d

8.

c _____ p

Say the word for each picture.
Find the picture that has the same middle sound as   .
Mark the ⬭ to show your answer.

9. ⬭

⬭

⬭

10. ⬭

⬭

⬭

Home Activity This page practices words that have the short a sound heard in *tap*. Work through the items with your child. Help your child make up fun rhymes using short a words, such as: *The fat cat in the black hat sat on the mat.*

Name_____

Pick a word from the box to finish each sentence.
Write the word on the line.

┌─────────────────────────────┐
│   I   like   the   │
└─────────────────────────────┘

1. _____ am a 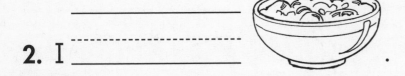 .

2. I _____ 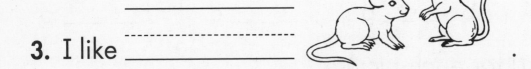 .

3. I like _____  .

4.  like _____ .

5. _____ like .

School + Home **Home Activity** This page helps your child learn to read and write the words *I*, *like*, and *the*. Work through the items with your child. Ask your child to use the words in sentences telling you things that he or she likes.

Name_____

Finish each sentence.
Write the words on the lines.

1.  like _____ .

2.  like _____ .

3. like _____ .

4. I like _____ .

5. I like _____ .

 Home Activity This page helps your child finish sentences and learn to write sentences. Help your child write the sentences. Then ask your child the things he or she may have in common with a pet, such as *like to play* and *need food and love.*

Practice Book Unit 1

Writing 5

Name_____

Say the word for each picture.
Circle the picture if the word begins
with the **s** sound heard in **seven**.

<u>s</u>even

1.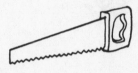

2.

3.

4.

5.

6.

7.

8.

9.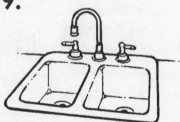

10.

11.

12.

© Pearson Education A

 Home Activity This page practices words that have the *s* sound heard in *soup*. Work through the items with your child. Then say aloud groups of three words, such as *cold*, *left*, and *safe*. Ask your child to listen carefully and name the word with the *s* sound.

Name_____

Say the word for each picture.
Circle the picture if the word begins
with the **p** sound heard in **pat**.   <u>p</u>at

1.

2.

3.

4.

5.

6.

7.

8.

9.

10.

11.

12.

 School + Home **Home Activity** This page practices words that have the *p* sound heard in *pink*. Work through the items with your child. Then act out words beginning with the *p* sound, such as *pig*, *pail*, *pat*, and *pet*, and have your child guess the word.

Name_____

Say the word for each picture.
Circle the word.

T<u>i</u>m

1.

map

pit

2.

sit

mat

3.

pat

mitt

4.

sip

Sam

Say the word for each picture.
Find the picture that has the same middle sound as .
Mark the ⬭ to show your answer.

5. ⬭ ⬭ ⬭

6. ⬭ ⬭ ⬭

---

7. ⬭ ⬭ ⬭

8. ⬭ ⬭ ⬭

School + Home

Home Activity This page practices words that have the short *i* sound heard in *ship*. Work through the items with your child. Have your child use the short *i* words pictured above in sentences.

Name_____

Pick a word from the box to finish each sentence.
Write it on the line.

a	is	look

1. Pip _____ a  .

2. Pip likes _____ 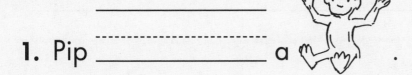 .

3. Pam _____ a 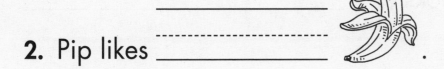 .

4. I _____ at Pam.

5. I _____ at Pip.

Home Activity This page helps your child learn to read and write the words *a*, *is*, and *look*. Work through the items with your child. Then help your child use these sentence frames to make more sentences: *Look at (name). (Name) is a _____.*

© Pearson Education A

Name_____

Finish each sentence.
Write the words on the lines.

1. A   is _____
_____
_____ .

2. A   looks at _____
_____
_____ .

3. A   likes _____
_____
_____ .

_____

4. I _____ .

_____

5. I _____ .

School + Home **Home Activity** This page helps your child finish sentences and learn to write sentences. Help your child write the sentences. Then ask your child to tell some ways he or she can help animals at home or at a shelter.

Name_____

Look for **C** and **c**.
Circle them.

Cc

1. D C O   **2.** B G C

3. c g e   **4.** o c p

Say the word for each picture.
Write c if you hear the sound of **c** heard in **camel**.

5.

_____
- - - - - - - - - - - -

6.

_____
- - - - - - - - - - - -

7.

_____
- - - - - - - - - - - -

8.

_____
- - - - - - - - - - - -

9.
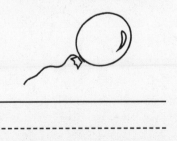
_____
- - - - - - - - - - - -

10.
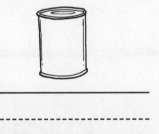
_____
- - - - - - - - - - - -

© Pearson Education A

Home Activity This page practices recognizing the letter *Cc* and identifying the sound of *c* heard in *cut*.
Say these words one at a time: *come, big, cake, cap, me*. Have your child stand up if the word starts with *c*.

Practice Book Unit 1   **Phonics Cc/k/ 11**

Name_____

Look for **B** and **b**.
Circle them.

Bb

1. B P D   **2.** E R B

3. p b q   **4.** d g b

Say the word for each picture.
Write b if you hear the sound of **b** heard in **bus**.

5.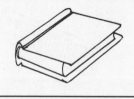

_____
- - - - - - - - - - -
_____

6.

_____
- - - - - - - - - - -
_____

7.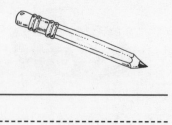

_____
- - - - - - - - - - -
_____

8.

_____
- - - - - - - - - - -
_____

9.

_____
- - - - - - - - - - -
_____

10.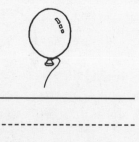

_____
- - - - - - - - - - -
_____

© Pearson Education A

School + Home

Home Activity This page practices recognizing the letter *Bb* and identifying the sound of *b* heard in *ball*. Work through the items with your child. Then help your child look at home for three things that begin with *b*.

Name_____

Look for **O** and **o**.
Circle them.   **Oo**

1. C   O   G   **2.** P   Q   O

3. g   o   c   **4.** o   e   d

Write o on each line.
Say the word you made.
Draw a line to the picture it matches.   c<u>o</u>t

5. m _____ p

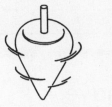

6. p _____ t

7. t _____ p

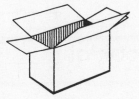

8. b _____ x

Home Activity This page practices recognizing the letter *Oo* and identifying the short *o* sound heard in *box*. Work through the items with your child. Then have your child spell these words: *top, Tom, mom, pot, Bob.*

© Pearson Education A

Name_____

Circle a word to finish each sentence.
Write it on the line.

We Have
_____

1. -------------------- look.

have you
_____

2. I -------------------- the cat.

have we
_____

3. I -------------------- the bat.

we   you
_____

4. I look at _____ .

Have We
_____

5. -------------------- like the top.

© Pearson Education A

School + Home **Home Activity** This page helps your child learn to read and write the words *have, you,* and *we.* Work through the items with your child. Then help your child make up sentences using the words *have, you,* and *we.*

14 **High-Frequency Words**   **Practice Book Unit 1**

Name_____

Think about how animals can help.
Finish the sentences.

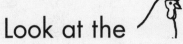

1. Look at the .

_____

It can _____ .

2. Look at the  .

_____

It can _____ .

3. Look at the _____ .

_____

It can _____ .

4. Look at the _____ .

_____

It can _____ .

© Pearson Education A

School + Home **Home Activity** This page helps your child learn to write sentences. Name each picture on the page. Then help your child write the sentences. Read the sentences together.

Practice Book Unit 1

Name_____

Look for **N** and **n**.
Circle them.

Nn

1. A N W   2. N M H

3. m u n   4. h n r

Say the word for each picture.
Write n if you hear the sound of **n** heard in **nickel**.

5.
_____
- - - - - - - - - - -
_____

6.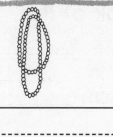
_____
- - - - - - - - - - -
_____

7.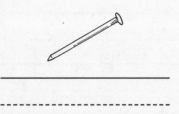
_____
- - - - - - - - - - -
_____

8.
_____
- - - - - - - - - - -
_____

9.
_____
- - - - - - - - - - -
_____

10.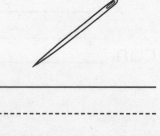
_____
- - - - - - - - - - -
_____

School + Home **Home Activity** This page practices recognizing the letter *Nn* and identifying the sound of *n* heard in *nurse*. For fun, let your child try saying this sentence quickly: *Nan needs nine nuts.* Then have him or her replace *nuts* with other words that begin with *n*.

© Pearson Education A

Name_____

Look for **D** and **d.**
Circle them.

Dd

1. P   R   D   **2.** B   O   D

3. p   d   g   **4.** d   q   b

Say the word for each picture. **Find** the picture that has the same beginning sound as  .
Mark the ⬭ to show your answer.

5.
   ⬭   ⬭

6.
   ⬭   ⬭

7.
   ⬭   ⬭

8.
   ⬭   ⬭

9.
   ⬭   ⬭

10.
   ⬭   ⬭

 School + Home **Home Activity** This page practices recognizing the letter *Dd* and identifying the sound of *d* heard in *dime*. Say the following words one at a time, and have your child say a rhyming word that begins with the *d* sound: *not, keep, may, rip.* (*dot, deep, day, dip*)

Name_____

Look for **R** and **r**.
Circle them.

Rr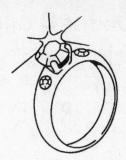

1. B P R   **2.** R D V

3. r n m   **4.** v h r

Say the word for each picture. **Find** the picture that has the same beginning sound as ⊙.
Mark the ⊂⊃ to show your answer.

5.
⊂⊃   ⊂⊃   ⊂⊃

6.
⊂⊃   ⊂⊃   ⊂⊃

7.
⊂⊃   ⊂⊃   ⊂⊃

8.
⊂⊃   ⊂⊃   ⊂⊃

 Home Activity This page practices recognizing the letter *Rr* and identifying the sound of *r* heard in *radio*. Say these pairs of words, and have your child say the word beginning with *r*: walk/run, rake/hoe, read/talk. Let your child act out the *r* word.

18 Phonics *Rr/r/*   **Practice Book Unit 1**

Name_____

Pick a word from the box to finish each sentence.
Write it on the line.

are	little	see

1. We _____ on a mat.

2. We _____ an ant.

3. The ant is _____ .

4. We _____ Dad.

5. Dad is not _____ .

© Pearson Education A

Home Activity This page helps your child learn to read and write the words *are*, *little*, and *see*. Work through the items together. Then write each word on a card. Lay the cards face down. Have your child pick up the cards and read the words.

Name_____

Finish each sentence. The words in the box may help you. **Write** the words on the lines.

sit   mat   nap   bib   little

1. I see  .

_____

The _____ are on a _____ .

2. I see .

_____

The have a _____ .

3. I see .

_____

The are _____ .

4. I see .

_____

The _____ in a .

5. I see .

_____

The _____ .

Home Activity This page helps your child practice writing sentences to describe animals. Help your child write the sentences. Then read them together. Have your child say a sentence describing another animal he or she has seen.

© Pearson Education A

Name_____

Look for **K** and **k**. **Circle** them.

Kk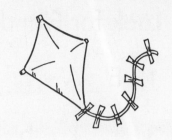

1. V K F   **2.** K H N

3. l k h   **4.** f y k

Say the word for each picture.
Find the picture that has
the same beginning sound as .
Mark the ⬭ to show your answer.

5.

6.

7.

8.

School + Home **Home Activity** This page practices recognizing the letter *Kk* and identifying the sound of *k* heard in *kitten*. Name each picture. Work through the items with your child. Say the following words one at a time, and have your child say a rhyming word that begins with *k: mitten, hid, fit, miss. (kitten, kid, kit, kiss)*

© Pearson Education A

Name_____

Look for F and f. Circle them.

Ff

1. L   A   F   2. P   F   B

3. f   k   b   4. d   h   f

Say the word for each picture.
Find the picture that has
the same beginning sound as  .
Mark the ⊂⊃ to show your answer.

5.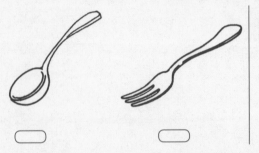

6.

7.

8.

9.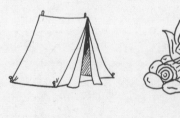

10.

 School + Home   **Home Activity** This page practices recognizing the letter *Ff* and identifying the sound of *f* heard in *finger*. Name each picture. Work through the items with your child. Then walk through your home with your child and ask him or her to point out things that begin with the *f* sound.

Name_____

Look for **E** and **e**.
Circle them.   **Ee**

1. E F P   **2.** B E R

3. e c o   **4.** b g e

Write e on each line.
Say the word you made.
Draw a line to the picture it matches.   h<u>e</u>n

5. b _____ d

6. p _____ n

7. n _____ t

8. t _____ n

© Pearson Education A

Home Activity This page practices recognizing the letter *Ee* and identifying the short *e* sound heard in *hen*. Work through the items with your child. Then write these words and ask your child to read them: *fed, met, pet, red, ten.*

Name_____

Circle a word to finish each sentence.
Write it on the line.

go   he
_____

1. Look at Min _____ !

they   go
_____

2. Look at Tom _____ !

He   They
_____

3. _____ run and run.

They   Go
_____

4. _____ sit on a mat.

Go   He
_____

5. _____ can fan Min.

School + Home **Home Activity** This page helps your child learn to read and write the words *go, he,* and *they.* Write *he, they, go, He, They,* and *Go* on cards. Lay the cards face down. Have your child pick up the cards one at a time and read each word.

© Pearson Education A

Name_____

Look at each picture. **Pick** a word from the box to finish each sentence. **Write** the word on the line.

| bed | fan | mat | net | pot |

1. I look on the _____ .

   I see a 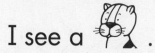 .

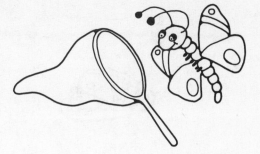

2. I look at the _____ .

   I see a 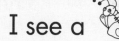 .

3. I look on the _____ .

   I see a  .

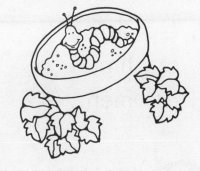

4. I look in the _____ .

   I see a 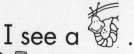 .

Home Activity This page helps your child finish sentences. After your child writes the missing words, read all the sentences together. Have your child say one more sentence for each picture.

© Pearson Education A

Name_____

Say the word for each picture.
Circle the word.

<u>h</u>en

---

1.  hit

has

2.  hot

hat

---

3.  hip

hand

4. hop

his

---

5.  ham

him

6. hot

hem

Find the word that has the same beginning sound
as . **Mark** the ⊖ to show your answer.

7. ⊖ hid
⊖ fit
⊖ not

8. ⊖ bad
⊖ red
⊖ had

9. ⊖ sip
⊖ him
⊖ men

10. ⊖ mad
⊖ hen
⊖ tap

© Pearson Education A

🏠 **School + Home** | **Home Activity** This page practices words that have the *h* sound heard in *home*. Work through the items with your child. Then say aloud groups of three words, such as *ten*, *head*, and *mend*. Ask your child to listen carefully and name the word with the *h* sound.

Name_____

Say the word for each picture.
Circle the picture if the word has
the **l** sound heard in **lid**.

lid →

1.

2.

3.

4.

5.

6.

7.

8.

9.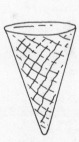

10.

11.

12.

© Pearson Education A

School + Home

Home Activity This page practices words that have the *l* sound heard in *light*. Work through the items with your child. Work together to write silly sentences using as many *l* words as possible. For example: *The laughing lizard licked the little lime.*

Practice Book Unit 1   **Phonics Ll/l/ 27**

Name_____

Say the word for each picture.
Write u on the line if you hear the
short **u** sound heard in **bus**.

b<u>u</u>s

1.

c ____ t

2.

s ____ n

3.

n ____ st

4.

t ____ b

5.

c ____ p

6.

n ____ t

7.

m ____ d

8.

b ____ nd

9.

p ____ p

10.

b ____ n

11.

p ____ t

12.

h ____ t

© Pearson Education A

School + Home

Home Activity This page practices words that have the short *u* sound heard in *bug*. Work through the items
with your child. Invite your child to write or say words that rhyme with *sun*.

Name_____

Pick a word from the box to finish each sentence.
Write it on the line.

Do	of	She

1. Fen sees lots _____  .

2. _____ looks at the  .

3. _____ the  see Fen?

4. Fen likes the skin _____ the  .

5. _____ likes the  best.

Home Activity This page helps your child learn to read and write the words *do, of,* and *she*. Work through the items with your child. Then help your child think of questions about animals that begin with the word *do*.

© Pearson Education A

Name_____

Finish each sentence.
Write the words on the lines.

_____
1. We can help _____ .

_____
2. We can _____ .

_____
3. We can help _____ .

_____
4. We can _____ .

5. Draw a picture of one way you can help animals.

Home Activity This page helps your child practice writing sentences. Work with your child to write the sentences. Then have your child name one kind of wild animal. Talk about different ways people might help this animal.

© Pearson Education A

Name_____

Pick letters from the box to finish each word.
Write the letters on the line.

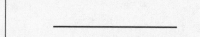

| fl | cl | cr | dr | sk | gr | sl | st | pl | sp |

1. _____ ed

2. _____ ap

3. _____ ot

4. _____ ip

5. _____ ag

6. _____ ar

7. _____ ab

8. _____ in

9. _____ ip

10. _____ um

© Pearson Education A

Home Activity This page practices words with initial consonant blends, such as *stop, play,* and *slant.* Name each picture. Work through the items with your child. Have your child say two words that begin with each blend on this page, such as *slide* and *slow* for the *sl* blend.

Name_____

Say the word for each picture.
Circle the letters that finish each word.
Write the letters on the line.   te**nt**

---

1. nt   st

ne _____

2. mp   nd

la _____

3. nd   lt

po _____

4. nt   nd

ha _____

---

5. mp   st

ju _____

6. lt   nt

be _____

7. nt   mp

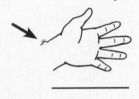

bu _____

8. nt   st

li _____

Find the word that has the same ending sound as the picture. **Mark** the ⬭ to show your answer.

9. ⬭ dent
⬭ last
⬭ sand

10. ⬭ left
⬭ fast
⬭ bend

Home Activity This page practices words with final consonant blends, such as *want*, *best*, and *land*. Work through the items with your child. Have your child make up sentences using words from this page.

© Pearson Education A

Name_____

Say the word for each picture.
Circle the picture if the word begins
with the **g** sound heard in **goat**.

goat

1.

2.

3.

4.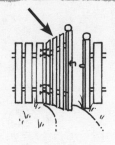

5.

6.

7.

8.

9.

10.

11.

12.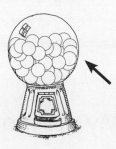

© Pearson Education A

School + Home
Home Activity This page practices words that have the *g* sound heard in *good*. Work through the items with your child. Invite him or her to find objects in your home that begin with the *g* sound.

Name_____

Pick a word from the box to finish each sentence.
Write it on the line.

| here   to   my |

_____
1. My dad is _____ .

_____
2. We like _____ fish in the pond.

_____
3. Here is _____ mom.

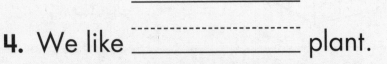

_____
4. We like _____ plant.

_____
5. My mom and _____ dad are fun!

© Pearson Education A

School + Home

Home Activity This page helps your child learn to read and write the words *here*, *to*, and *my*. Work through the items with your child. Then have your child use the words *my* and *to* in sentences that tell things he or she likes doing with your family.

Name_____

Finish each sentence.
Write the words on the lines.

What does your family do together?

_____

1. We like to _____ .

_____

2. We like to _____ .

_____

3. We go to _____ .

_____

4. We go to _____ .

5. Draw a picture of your family.

Home Activity This page helps your child finish sentences and learn to write sentences. Help your child write the sentences. Then ask your child his or her favorite things to do with your family. Plan a special family trip together!

© Pearson Education A

Name_____

Say the word for each picture.
Write w on the line if you hear the **w** sound
heard in **well**.

<u>w</u>ell

1.
_____
_____ et

2.
_____
_____ ig

3.
_____
_____ rog

4.
_____
_____ eb

5.
_____
_____ ind

6.
_____
_____ ag

7.
_____
_____ an

8.
_____
_____ en

Find the word that begins with the **w** sound heard in ▦.
Mark the ⬭ to show your answer.

9. ⬭ mask
   ⬭ will
   ⬭ fist

10. ⬭ flag
    ⬭ bell
    ⬭ went

School + Home **Home Activity** This page practices words that have the *w* sound heard in *west*. Work through the items with your child. Then work with him or her to make words that rhyme with *will* and *wig*.

Practice Book Unit 2

Name_____

Say the word for each picture.
Circle the picture if the word begins with
the **j** sound heard in **jet**.

<u>j</u>et

1. 	**2.** 	**3.** 	**4.** 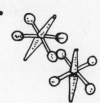
5. 	**6.** 	**7.** 	**8.** 

Pick a word from the box to finish each sentence.
Write it on the line.

> **job**   **jog**   **jet**

9. I help dogs and cats. It is my _____ .

10. Look up! I am in a _____ .

Home Activity This page practices words that have the *j* sound heard in *just*. Work through the items with your child. Then with your child, search for things around your home that begin with the *j* sound, such as *jar, jelly, jug,* or *jeans.*

Name_____

Say the word for each picture.
Circle the word.

wa<u>x</u>

---

1. 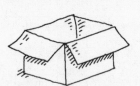   box

bend

2.    fat

fox

---

3.    sip

six

4.   ax

at

---

5.    mix

map

6.    fist

fix

---

7.    ax

ox

8.    sad

sax

Find the word that has the same ending sound as .
Mark the ⬭ to show your answer.

9. ⬭ flex
　　 ⬭ flip
　　 ⬭ test

10. ⬭ dust
　　 ⬭ stand
　　 ⬭ tax

© Pearson Education A

Home Activity This page practices words that have the *x* sound heard in *wax*. Name each picture. Work through the items with your child. Then help your child make up a story about a fox in a box.

Name_____

Pick a word from the box to finish each sentence.
Write it on the line.

> one   two   three

1. Ann has _____ pals.

2. They have _____ pets.

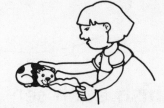

3. The best _____ is Spot.

4. Spot likes to sit in _____ big box.

5. Spot has _____ pals just like Ann.

 Home Activity This page helps your child learn to read and write the words *one*, *two*, and *three*. Work through the items with your child. Then help your child write *one*, *two*, *three*, *1*, *2*, and *3* on separate index cards. Have him or her match the number words with the numerals.

Name_____

Write the name of something you can share with your friends in each circle.

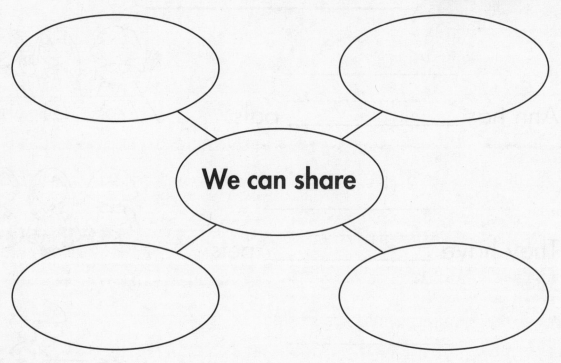

We can share

Finish each sentence. The words in the web may help you. **Write** the words on the lines.

1. We can share _____ .

2. We can share _____ .

© Pearson Education A

Home Activity This page helps your child finish sentences and learn to write sentences. Help your child write the sentences. Then have your child tell you some things he or she shares with friends.

Name_____

Say the word for each picture.
Circle the picture if the word begins
with the **v** sound heard in **van**.

<u>v</u>an

1.

2.

3.

4.

5.

6.

7.

8.

9.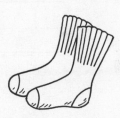

10.

11.

12.

© Pearson Education A

 Home Activity This page practices words that have the *v* sound heard in *valley*. Work through the items with your child. Then have your child use the word for each circled picture above in a sentence.

Name_____

Say the word for each picture.
Circle the word to finish each sentence.
Write it on the line.

<u>z</u>ebra

buzz   bust

_____

1. Bugs like to _____ .

jump   jazz

_____

2. The disk is _____ .

zip   zap

_____

3. I can _____ up my vest.

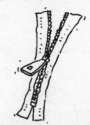

flop   fuzz

_____

4. Puff has soft _____ .

fizz   fit

_____

5. Can you see the _____ ?

© Pearson Education A

School + Home **Home Activity** This page practices words that have the z sound heard in *zoo*. Work through the items with your child. Then ask your child to tell you two words that start with the z sound and two words that end with the z sound.

Name _____

Pick a word from the box to match each picture.
Write it on the line.

yam yell yak yes yo-yo yap yank you

1.

_____

2.

_____

3.

_____

4.

_____

5.

_____

6.

_____

7.

_____

8.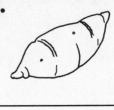

_____

Find the word that has the **y** sound heard in .
Mark the ⬭ to show your answer.

9. ⬭ yet

⬭ went

⬭ van

10. ⬭ pest

⬭ yelp

⬭ men

Home Activity This page practices words that have the *y* sound heard in *year*. Work through the items with your child. Ask your child to tell you the beginning sound in *yellow*. Then have him or her point out yellow objects in your home or neighborhood.

© Pearson Education A

Name_____

Name_____

Pick a word from the box to finish each sentence.
Write it on the line.

from	me	said

1. Brett is _____ my ball club.

2. He helps _____ hit the ball.

3. My vet Nan is _____ here.

4. Nan _____ she will help Kit.

5. Kit can help _____ !

School + Home

Home Activity This page helps your child learn to read and write the words *from*, *me*, and *said*. Work through the items with your child. Then help your child write the words on index cards and practice reading them.

Name_____

Finish each sentence.
Write the words on the lines.

_____

1. Here is the _____ .

_____

2. He helps _____ .

_____

3. Here is _____ .

_____

4. She helps _____ .

Finish the sentence.
Tell something you do to help.

_____

5. I help _____ .

Home Activity This page helps your child finish sentences and learn to write sentences. Help your child write the sentences. Then talk with your child about what your family can do to be good neighbors. Write a list and put it on the refrigerator.

Practice Book Unit 2

Writing 45

Name_____

Pick a word from the box to finish each sentence.
Write it on the line.

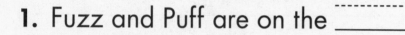

| quiz | quilt | quiet | quit |

1. Fuzz and Puff are on the _____ .

2. Little Dan is _____ in his crib.

3. Tag must _____ !

4. Jill has a _____ in class.

Animals talk in different ways. **Say** the word for the sound each animal makes. **Circle** the animal whose sound begins with the q sound heard in .

5.

Home Activity This page practices words that have the q sound heard in *quick*. Work through the items with your child. Then have your child read the words in the box and use each word in a spoken sentence.

© Pearson Education A

Name_____

Say the word for each picture.
Circle the word.

du**ck**

1.

list

lick

2.

clip

clock

3.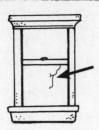

crack

crab

4.

past

pack

5.

stamp

sack

6.

back

bad

7.

stick

stand

8.

jab

jack

9.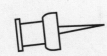

task

tack

10.

sock

stop

© Pearson Education A

Home Activity This page practices words that end with the sound heard in *rack*. Name each picture and work through the items with your child. Then work together to make up silly sentences about ducks using words ending with *ck*, such as: *The duck wore a pack on his back.*

Name_____

Say the word for each picture.
Circle the word.

pig<u>s</u>

---

1.  hat

hats

2.  lamp

lamps

---

3.   bug

bugs

4.   duck

ducks

---

5.  cup

cups

6.  lock

locks

---

7.  sled

sleds

8.  ant

ants

Find the word that means more than one.
Mark the ⬭ to show your answer.

9. ⬭ dress
⬭ gas
⬭ pins

10. ⬭ is
⬭ kids
⬭ has

© Pearson Education A

School + Home **Home Activity** This page practices words that end with *-s* and mean more than one. Work through the items with your child. Help your child name things in your home of which you have more than one, such as *shirts*, *socks*, *pets*, *chairs*, and *apples*. Emphasize the *-s* ending.

Name_____

Pick a word from the box to finish each sentence.
Write it on the line.

for   was   what

1. The cub _____ little.
   _____

2. They can look _____ fish in the pond.
   _____

3. Here is _____ Mom can do.
   _____

4. Here is _____ Dad can do.
   _____

5. They can run just _____ fun!
   _____

© Pearson Education A

Home Activity This page helps your child learn to read and write the words *for, was,* and *what.*
Work through the items with your child. Then take turns with your child finishing these sentences:
What can I do for ...? I can ...

Practice Book Unit 2   **High-Frequency Words** **49**

Name_____

Look at the pictures. **Finish** each sentence.
Write the words on the lines.

1. They all have _____ .

2. They all have _____ .

3. They all can _____ .

4. They all can _____ .

5. **Draw** a picture of your family working together.

© Pearson Education A

Home Activity This page helps your child finish sentences and learn to write sentences. Help your child write the sentences. Then ask your child the things your family may have in common with animal families, such as: *We play together. We eat together.*

Name_____

Add -s to each word.
Write the new word on the line.

1. hop _____

2. nap _____

3. get _____   4. see _____   5. help _____

Use the words you wrote to finish the sentences.
Write the words on the lines.

6. The bug _____ a big plant.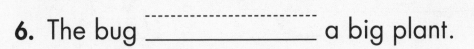

7. The bug _____ up the stem.

8. He _____ on top in the sun.

9. The bug _____ wet.

10. The plant _____ the wet bug.

© Pearson Education A

 School + Home **Home Activity** This page practices action words that end with -s, such as *jogs*. Work through the items with your child. Help your child think of different action words, such as *runs, hops, skips,* and *jumps,* and then have him or her act out each word.

Name_____

Add -ing to each word.
Write the new word on the line.

1. look _____

2. snack _____

3. do _____ 4. go _____ 5. jump _____

Use the words you wrote to finish the sentences.
Write the words on the lines.

6. What is Pig _____ ?

7. Pig is _____ in the plants!

8. Pig is _____ on my plants!

9. He is _____ at the bugs.

10. Pig is _____ back in his pen!

School + Home **Home Activity** This page practices words that end with -ing, such as helping. Work through the items with your child. Help your child write look, jump, go, do, and -ing on index cards. Then have him or her add -ing to each action word and read it aloud.

Practice Book Unit 2

Name_____

Circle a word to finish each sentence.
Write it on the line.

yellow   yell

_____

1. The sun is _____ .

---

glass   green

_____

2. My cat likes _____ grass.

---

green   grab

_____

3. The skunk sits next to a _____ plant.

---

yet   yellow

_____

4. He snacks on a _____ cob.

---

blue   belt

_____

5. The pup snacks on a _____ sock.
Bad pup!

 School + Home **Home Activity** This page helps your child learn to read and write the words *blue, green,* and *yellow.* Work through the items with your child. Then have your child point out objects that are blue, green, and yellow.

Name_____

Finish each sentence.
Write the words on the lines.

1. Plants help  get _____ .
   _____

2. Plants help  get _____ .
   _____

3. Plants help  get _____ .
   _____

4. Plants help  get _____ .
   _____

5. Plants help  and
   _____
   get _____ .

Home Activity This page helps your child finish sentences and learn to write sentences. Help your child write the sentences. Then ask your child to tell you ways plants help people, such as: *Plants give people food.*

© Pearson Education A

Name_____

Pick a word from the box to match each picture.
Write it on the line.

net	frog	pup	mitt	spot	hill
flag	bell	tag	buzz	bed	drip

1.

_____

- - - - - - - - - - - -

2.

_____

- - - - - - - - - - - -

3.

_____

- - - - - - - - - - - -

4.

_____

- - - - - - - - - - - -

5.

_____

- - - - - - - - - - - -

6.

_____

- - - - - - - - - - - -

7.

_____

- - - - - - - - - - - -

8.

_____

- - - - - - - - - - - -

9.

_____

- - - - - - - - - - - -

10.

_____

- - - - - - - - - - - -

11.

_____

- - - - - - - - - - - -

12.

_____

- - - - - - - - - - - -

© Pearson Education A

Home Activity This page practices words that have consonant and vowel letter patterns, such as *pet, stop,* and *well.* Name each picture. Work through the items with your child. Then help your child think of words that rhyme with the words on this page.

Practice Book Unit 2

Phonics Short Vowel Word Families **55**

Name_____

Pick a word to finish each sentence. Write it on the line.

What   Where
_____

1. _____ is my hot dog?

Come   Clip
_____

2. _____ here and see!

___

pot   put
_____

3. Buzz _____ a little bug on her lap.

was   where
_____

4. Here is _____ she has a nap.

___

come   crab
_____

5. Ants _____ to get a snack.

pit   put
_____

6. They will _____ it on his back.

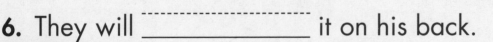

Home Activity This page helps your child learn to read and write the words *come, put,* and *where*. Work through the items with your child. Then have him or her ask questions beginning with the word *where*.

Name_____

Think of ways kids can help.
Think of ways bugs can help.
Write the words in the chart.

Kids can	**Bugs can**
_____	_____
_____	_____
_____	_____
_____	_____
_____	_____

Use words from the chart to finish the sentences.
Write the words on the lines.

_____

1. Kids can _____ .

_____

2. Kids can _____ .

_____

3. Bugs can _____ .

_____

4. Bugs can _____ .

Home Activity This page helps your child learn to finish sentences. Help your child write the sentences. Have your child act out things he or she can do around the house. Have your child say what he or she is doing, such as: *I can set the table.*

Name_____

Circle the correct word for each picture.

shed

1.  shell
   sell

2.  cash
   can

3.  drip
   ship

4.  fish
   fill

5.  shin
   stick

6.  brush
   brick

7.  stop
   shop

8. 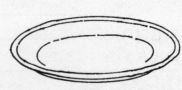 dig
   dish

© Pearson Education A

Home Activity This page practices words with the *sh* sound. Work through the items with your child. Then help your child write these words and tell what they mean: *dish, shin, shell,* and *brush.*

58 **Phonics** Digraph *sh*   **Practice Book Unit 3**

Name_____

Read the word.
Circle the correct picture
for each word.   **th**ey

---

1. thick

2. bath

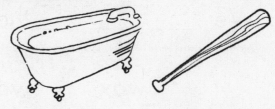

---

3. thin

4. three

---

5. cloth

6. path

Find the word that has the same beginning sound as .
Mark the ⬭ to show your answer.

7. ⬭ pick
  ⬭ thick
  ⬭ sick

8. ⬭ bank
  ⬭ tank
  ⬭ thank

© Pearson Education A

Home Activity This page practices words with the *th* sound. Work through the items with your child. Then have your child write these words and tell what they mean: *thump, math,* and *cloth.*

Practice Book Unit 3   **Phonics** Digraph *th* **59**

Name_____

Circle a word to finish each sentence.
Write it on the line.

b**all**

call   cat

_____

1. We _____ the dogs.

wax   walk

_____

2. The dogs _____ to us.

all   add

_____

3. We _____ pet the dogs.

talk   tack

_____

4. Mom can _____ to the dogs.

bell   ball

_____

5. The dogs see a _____ .

Home Activity This page practices words with the *a* sound that is heard in *ball* and *talk*. Work through the items with your child. Help your child write these words that rhyme: *all, ball, call, fall, hall, tall,* and *wall.*

60 **Phonics** Vowel Sound in *ball*   **Practice Book Unit 3**

© Pearson Education A

Name_____

Look at the picture. **Circle** the answer to each question.
Hint: One question will have
two answers.

1. What has a hat?   the dog   the cat

2. What has a ball?   the dog   the cat

3. What has legs?   the dog   the cat

4. What is big?   the dog   the cat

5. What is little?   the dog   the cat

Nat   Deb   Pat

6. Which two dogs are the same?

_____   _____

- - - - - - - - - - - - - - -   - - - - - - - - - - - - - - -

_____   _____

7. Which dog is not like the others?

_____

- - - - - - - - - - - - - - -

_____

Home Activity This page helps your child identify how animal characters are alike and different. Work through the items with your child. Then ask your child to tell how the dog Deb is different from Nat and Pat.

Name_____

Pick a word from the box to finish each sentence.
Write it on the line.

her	now	use

1. The man can _____ the pen.

2. He is _____ dad.

3. They will go _____ .

4. He can see _____ .

5. Come here _____ .

Home Activity This page helps your child learn to read and write the words *her, now,* and *use.* Work through the items with your child. For practice, have your child look at each word in the box, read it, and spell it.

© Pearson Education A

Name_____

Finish each sentence. **Write** the words on the lines.
The words in the box may help you.

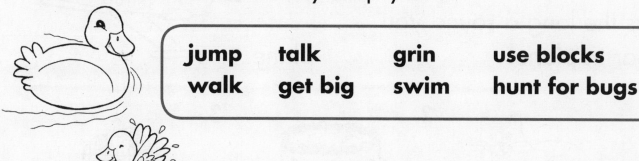

jump	talk	grin	use blocks
walk	get big	swim	hunt for bugs

1. A duck can _____ .

2. I can _____ .

3. I can _____ .

4. A duck and I can _____ .

5. Write a sentence about what ducks can do.

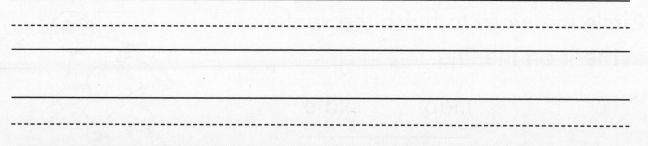

_____

_____

_____

Home Activity This page helps your child finish sentences and learn to write sentences. Help your child write the sentences. Then read them together.

Name_____

Say the word for each picture.
Circle the picture if the word
has the long **a** sound you
hear in **plane.**

pl**a**n**e**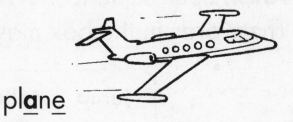

---

1.  | 2.  | 3.

---

4.  | 5. 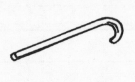 | 6.

---

7.  | 8.  | 9.

Circle the word to finish the sentence.
Write it on the line.

map   skate

10. Ben likes to _____ .

Home Activity This page practices words with the long *a* sound. Work through the items with your child.
Help your child list two or three words that rhyme with *skate* and *wave*.

© Pearson Education A

Name_____

Say the word for each picture.
Write c on the line if you hear the
c sound as in **lace.**

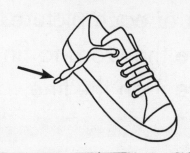

la<u>c</u>e

1.

_____
- - - - - - - - -
_____ ent

2.

_____
- - - - - - - - -
ra _____ e

3.

_____
- - - - - - - - -
du _____

4.

_____
- - - - - - - - -
_____ ity

5.

_____
- - - - - - - - -
la _____ e

6.

_____
- - - - - - - - -
fa _____ e

Find the word that has the same
sound as **c** in **city.**
Mark the ⬭ to show your answer.

7. ⬭ tack
⬭ cell
⬭ bake

8. ⬭ can
⬭ hop
⬭ lace

Home Activity This page practices words with the c sound heard in *race.* Work through the items with your child. Then have your child write these words and tell what they mean: *place, space, lace.*

© Pearson Education A

Name_____

Look at each picture.
Circle the word to finish each sentence.
Write it on the line.

gem

age   wag   nap
_____
- - - - - - - - - - - - - - - - - - -

1. Lin's _____ is six.

egg   gap   stage
_____
- - - - - - - - - - - - - - - - - - -

2. She can sing on the _____ .

cap   cage   gate
_____
- - - - - - - - - - - - - - - - - - -

3. Jon can see a _____ .

hall   gem   dog
_____
- - - - - - - - - - - - - - - - - - -

4. He can see a _____ .

page   grape   pan
_____
- - - - - - - - - - - - - - - - - - -

5. Lin and Jon read the _____ .

Home Activity This page practices words with the *g* sound heard in *rage*. Work through the items with your child. Help your child write these words and use each in a sentence: *stage, age,* and *page.*

Name_____

Look at the pictures.
Circle the answer to each question.

1. Who has a pet?   Kate   Shane

2. Who can read?   Kate   Shane

3. Who is with her mom?   Kate   Shane

4. Who gets help?   Kate   Shane

5. Who is little?   Kate   Shane

6. Who sits by a gate?   Kate   Shane

7. Draw two faces that are the same.

8. Draw two faces that are different.

School + Home **Home Activity** This page helps your child identify how two people are different. Work through the items with your child. Then ask your child to show different faces that people can make, like happy or sad faces.

Practice Book Unit 3   **Comprehension** Compare and Contrast **67**

Name_____

Pick a word from the box to finish each sentence.
Write it on the line.

old	too	want

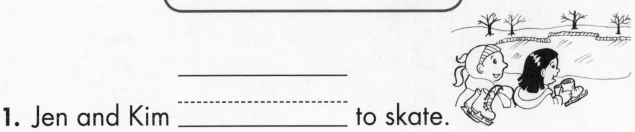

1. Jen and Kim _____ to skate.

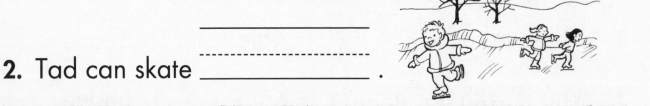

2. Tad can skate _____ .

3. They _____ to help Tad.

4. Jen has _____ skates.

5. Pup wants to play _____ .

Home Activity This page helps your child learn to read and write the words *old, too,* and *want*. Work through the items with your child. Help your child make up a story about the snow using these words.

68 **High-Frequency Words** **Practice Book Unit 3**

© Pearson Education A

Name_____

Finish each sentence. **Write** the words on the lines. The words in the box may help you.

smile	spell	get help
hit a ball	make a mess	run a race

1. A baby can not _____ .

2. A baby can _____

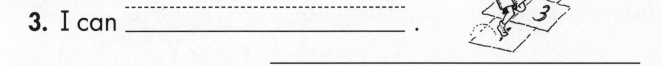

3. I can _____ .

4. A baby and I can _____ .

5. **Write** a sentence about what you can do now that you are big. Write your sentence on the lines.

_____

_____

_____

Home Activity This page helps your child finish sentences and learn to write sentences. Help your child write the sentences. Then help your child think of more things he or she can do now.

Name_____

Circle the word for each picture.

m<u>i</u>ce

1. 	five face	2. 	back bike
3.	dim dime	4. 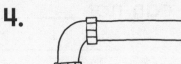	pipe pin
5. 	kite kick	6. 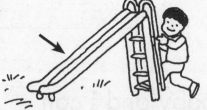	slip slide
7. 	smile snake	8. 	lime lid
9. 	vase vine	10. 	hive had

Home Activity This page practices words with the long *i* sound. Work through the items with your child. Help your child make flashcards of some long *i* words. Have your child practice reading the words.

Name_____

Read the word.
Circle the correct picture for
each word.

whisk

---

1. whale

2. whip

Circle a word to finish each sentence.
Write it on the line.

When   They

_____

3. _____ can we go?

talk   whack

_____

4. Tim can _____ the ball.

Find the word that has the same sound as **wh** in **when**.
Mark the ⬭ to show your answer.

5. ⬭ whiff
   ⬭ shine
   ⬭ that

6. ⬭ fish
   ⬭ hole
   ⬭ whack

© Pearson Education A

Home Activity This page practices words with the *wh* sound heard in *while*. Work through the items with
your child. Then have your child write these words and use each in a sentence: *whale, when, while.*

Name_____

Read the word.
Circle the picture
for each word.

check  wa**tch**

1. catch

2. chest

3. patch

4. chin

5. match

6. chop

Find the word that has the same sound as **ch** in **mu<u>ch</u>**.
Mark the ⬭ to show your answer.

7. ⬭ wake
⬭ ditch
⬭ ship

8. ⬭ city
⬭ chill
⬭ cape

© Pearson Education A

School + Home

Home Activity This page practices words with the *ch* sound heard in *pitch*. Work through the items with your child. Help your child write these words and practice reading them aloud: *chip, pitch, chill, chick, watch, itch, rich, chase.*

Name_____

Look at the pictures.
Circle the answer to
each question.
Hint: One question will
have two answers.

Ana   Mike

1. Who will pitch?   Ana   Mike

2. Who has a bike?   Ana   Mike

3. Who has a ball?   Ana   Mike

4. Who has stripes?   Ana   Mike

5. Who rides the bike?   Ana   Mike

6. Who can have fun?   Ana   Mike

7. Write one way that Ana and Mike are the same.

_____

_____

8. Write one way that Ana and Mike are not the same.

_____

_____

© Pearson Education A

Home Activity This page helps your child identify how two characters are the same and different. Work through the items with your child. Then have your child tell more ways that the characters are the same or different.

Practice Book Unit 3   **Comprehension** Compare and Contrast **73**

Name_____

Pick a word from the box to finish each sentence.
Write it on the line.

> there   who   your

_____
1. _____ will go on the trip?

2. The bus is here for _____ trip.

3. The pet shop is _____ .

4. This is the man _____ helps the pets.

5. The dogs are _____ .

School + Home **Home Activity** This page helps your child learn to read and write the words *there, who,* and *your.* Work through the items with your child. Then ask your child to write the words and read them aloud.

© Pearson Education A

Name_____

Finish each sentence. **Write** the words on the lines. The words in the box may help you.

run	jump	swim	sit
cats	dogs	fish	pets
glad	smile	sad	look

1. A little pet can _____ .

2. I like little _____ .

3. A little pet makes me _____ .

4. When it is big, it will _____ .

5. Then I will _____ .

6. Draw a picture of a pet.

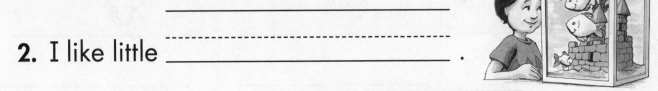
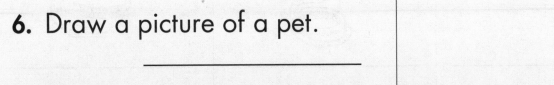

This is a _____ .

Home Activity This page helps your child finish sentences and learn to write sentences. Help your child write words in the sentences. Then discuss how living things can grow.

Practice Book Unit 3 **Writing 75**

© Pearson Education A

Name_____

Write a word from the box to match each picture.

bone	nose
rope	stone
robe	smoke
hose	note
rose	

cone

1.

_____

2.

_____

3.

_____

4.

_____

5.

_____

6.

_____

7.

_____

8.

_____

9.

_____

Home Activity This page practices words with the long *o* sound. Work through the items with your child. Then help your child make up a rhyme using the words *rose, nose,* and *those.*

Name_____

Read each sentence.
Circle the contraction for the underlined words.

I will come with you.   I'll come with you.

1. You will find the garden.   You'll   Hasn't

2. The bug was not here.   wasn't   didn't

3. I can not pick the bud.   aren't   can't

4. We will smell the rose.   We'll   Wasn't

5. The bugs are not big.   haven't   aren't

© Pearson Education A

School + Home   **Home Activity** This page practices contractions with *'ll* and *n't*. Work through the items with your child. Then say a contraction, such as *didn't*. Have your child tell the two words that were combined to make the contraction.

Name_____

Write the contraction for each pair of words.

1. is not   _____

2. had not   _____

I am here for the game.
I'm here for the game.

3. I am   _____

4. he will   _____

5. was not   _____

6. they will   _____

7. I will   _____

8. did not   _____

Find the contraction.

Mark the ⬭ to show your answer.

9. ⬭ am   10. ⬭ has
   ⬭ I'm   ⬭ have
   ⬭ I am   ⬭ hasn't

Home Activity This page practices contractions with 'm, 'll, and n't, such as I'm, I'll, and can't. Work through the items with your child. Then help your child write he, she, I, you, we, am, not, and will on index cards and make contractions.

78 **Phonics** Contractions 'm, 'll, and n't   **Practice Book Unit 3**

Name_____

Look at the pictures.
Write 1, 2, 3 to put the sentences in order.

_____

1. At last plants can grow. _____

_____

2. The snow is cold. _____

_____

3. The hot sun melts the snow. _____

_____

4. The bug lands on the rose. _____

_____

5. First there is a rose. _____

_____

6. Then the bug takes a nap. _____

 Home Activity This page helps your child put events in order to form a story. Work through the items with your child. Then ask your child to draw a series of pictures showing three events in the order in which they happen.

© Pearson Education A

Name_____

Pick a word from the box to finish each sentence.
Write it on the line.

could   eat   very

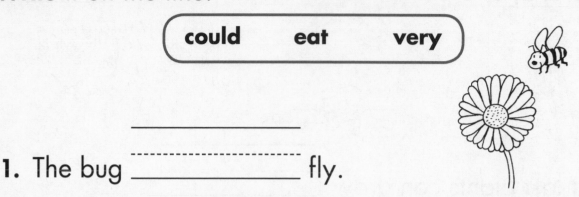

_____
1. The bug _____ fly.

_____
2. This bug will _____ the plant.

_____
3. The wind is _____ cold.

_____
4. The roses _____ go there.

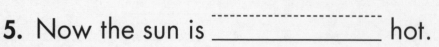

_____
5. Now the sun is _____ hot.

 Home Activity This page helps your child learn to read and write the words *could, eat,* and *very.* Work through the items with your child. Then have your child use each word in a sentence about how seasons change each year.

Name_____

Finish each sentence. **Write** the words on the lines. The words in the box may help you.

| dig holes | pop up | get big | eat plants |
| help plants | can hide | kill plants | |

1. The sun helps plants _____ .

2. Some bugs _____ .

3. Bad bugs _____ .

Write two sentences about what you can do in a garden. Write your sentences on the lines.

4. _____

_____

5. _____

_____

Home Activity This page helps your child finish sentences and learn to write sentences. Help your child write the sentences. Then have your child think up a story about bugs.

Name_____

Circle the correct word for each picture.

St<u>e</u>v<u>e</u>    m<u>u</u>l<u>e</u>

1. 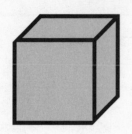 cube

cub

2.  tub

tube

3.  duck

duke

4. pet

Pete

5. cut

cute

6.  cub

cube

7.  egg

Eve

8. fluff

flute

© Pearson Education A

 Home Activity This page practices words with the long *u* and long *e* sounds, as in *mule* and *Steve*. Work through the items with your child. Then say these words and names, and have your child find them on the page: *tube, Pete, cute, Eve,* and *mule*.

Name_____

Pick a word from the box
to match each picture.
Write it on the line.

b<u>ee</u>

| feet he queen she sheep tree |

1.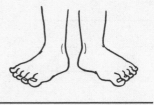
_____
- - - - - - - - - - - - - - -
_____

2.
_____
- - - - - - - - - - - - - - -
_____

3.
_____
- - - - - - - - - - - - - - -
_____

4.
_____
- - - - - - - - - - - - - - -
_____

5.
_____
- - - - - - - - - - - - - - -
_____

6.
_____
- - - - - - - - - - - - - - -
_____

Find the word that has the same vowel sound as .
Mark the ⬭ to show your answer.

7. ⬭ me
   ⬭ met
   ⬭ mat

8. ⬭ wed
   ⬭ wad
   ⬭ weed

Home Activity This page practices words with the long *e* sound spelled *e* or *ee*, as in *me* and *keep*. Work through the items with your child. Then have your child say a rhyming word for these words: *need, beep, peel, we,* and *sheet.*

© Pearson Education A

Practice Book Unit 3

Phonics Long *e: e, ee* **83**

Name_____

Look at the pictures.
Write 1, 2, 3 to put the sentences in order.

_____

1. Dan and Frank catch a fish. _____

_____

2. Dan and Frank sit by the lake. _____

_____

3. Dan feels a tug. _____

_____

4. Min puts on her skates. _____

_____

5. Min skates from place to place. _____

_____

6. Min gets two skates. _____

 Home Activity This page helps your child put events in order to form a story. Work through the items with your child. Then have your child tell about something that happened at school. Ask what happened first, next, and last.

© Pearson Education A

84 **Comprehension** Sequence   **Practice Book Unit 3**

Name_____

Pick a word from the box to finish each sentence.
Write it on the line.

| good | out | saw |

1. The dog _____ Kent.

2. The dog went _____ to play.

3. Kent _____ his dog in the grass.

4. Kent came _____ too.

5. Kent and his pet had a _____ time!

School + Home

Home Activity This page helps your child learn to read and write the words *good*, *out*, and *saw*. Work through the items with your child. Then have your child close his or her eyes and spell the words as you say them.

Name_____

Find words to finish each sentence. **Write** the words on the line. The words in the box may help you.

can	walk	has	swim	big
small	legs	is	see	

1. A baby frog can _____
   _____.

2. A baby frog
   gets big. The frog _____
   _____.

3. A baby snake _____
   _____.

4. A baby snake
   gets big. The snake _____
   _____.

5. A baby _____
   _____.

6. The baby gets
   to be a kid. The kid _____
   _____.

Home Activity This page gives practice in finishing sentences. Help your child write the sentences. Then read them together. Ask your child to name one way he or she has changed while growing.

Name_____

Pick a word from the box to finish each sentence.
Add **-ed** to each word. **Write** it on the line.

walk   play   look   help   dress

1. Al woke up and got _____ .

2. He _____ to school with Jan.

3. Al _____ at two books.

4. He _____ a game at lunch.

5. Al _____ Lee with math.

 School + Home **Home Activity** This page practices writing words that end in *-ed*, such as *walked*. Work through the items with your child. Then ask your child to read the words he or she wrote and use each one in a new sentence.

© Pearson Education A

Name_____

Circle the word for each picture.

ra**bb**it

1.

pump
puppet

2.

mitten
mint

3.

walnut
wall

4.

button
bump

5.

kite
kitten

6.

walrus
wall

7.

picnic
pick

8.

munch
muffin

Write the word for each picture.

9.

basket
base

10.

hello
helmet

_____

- - - - - - - - - - - - - -

_____

_____

- - - - - - - - - - - - - -

_____

School + Home **Home Activity** This page gives practice reading words with two syllables that have two consonants in the middle. Work through the items with your child. Then have your child choose three of the circled words and use each in a sentence.

© Pearson Education A

Name_____

Write 1, 2, 3 in each row to show the right order.

1. ☐

2. ☐

3. ☐

4. ☐

5. ☐

6. ☐

Draw a picture to show what happens next.
Write a sentence about your picture.

7.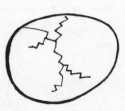

_____
- - - - - - - - - - - - - -
_____
_____
- - - - - - - - - - - - - -
_____

© Pearson Education A

 Home Activity This page gives your child practice putting pictures in order to form a story. Have your child choose one of the scenes from above. Then help your child write sentences that tell what happened first, next, and last in the story.

Practice Book Unit 3　　　　**Comprehension Sequence 89**

Name_____

Pick a word from the box to finish each sentence.
Write it on the line.

| down | way | work |

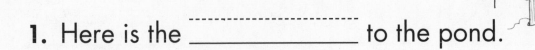

1. Here is the _____ to the pond.

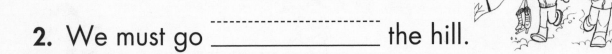

2. We must go _____ the hill.

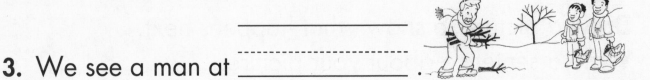

3. We see a man at _____ .

4. This is the _____ to skate.

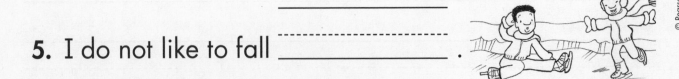

5. I do not like to fall _____ .

Home Activity This page helps your child learn to read and write the words *down*, *way*, and *work*. Read the items with your child. Write the three words on cards. Then take turns drawing two cards at a time. Use both words in one sentence.

© Pearson Education A

Name_____

Write an answer to each question.
The words in the box may help you.

green buds	kids with rakes	school bus	sun
kids on bikes	tall grass	roses	ice
kids in hats	kids swim	bugs	

1. What can you see in spring?

_____

I can see _____ .

2. What can you see in summer?

_____

I can see _____ .

3. What can you see in fall?

_____

I can see _____ .

4. What can you see in winter?

_____

I can see _____ .

5. What is the best time of year?

_____

I think _____ .

 Home Activity This page gives practice in writing sentences to answer questions. Help your child write the sentences. Then read them together. Ask your child to name three things that can be seen during his or her favorite season.

© Pearson Education A

Name_____

Circle a word to finish each sentence.
Write it on the line.

fl<u>y</u>

---

my   met
_____
- - - - - - - - - - -

1. I walk with _____ cat.

---

be   by
_____
- - - - - - - - - - -

2. We sit _____ a tree.

---

skip   sky
_____
- - - - - - - - - - -

3. We look up at the _____.

---

try   tap
_____
- - - - - - - - - - -

4. We will _____ to run fast.

---

dry   drip
_____
- - - - - - - - - - -

5. We like to be _____.

© Pearson Education A

School + Home

Home Activity This page practices words with the long *i* sound of *y*, as in *fly* or *try*. Work through the items with your child. Then talk about these words and help your child write them: *fry*, *cry*, *shy*, and *spy*.

Circle the correct word for each picture.

penn**y**

1.    puppy

put

2.   jeep

jelly

3.    sum

sunny

4.    happy

hatch

5. **20**   twenty

try

6.    mommy

mitten

7.    bump

bunny

8.    must

muddy

Find the word that has the same **y** sound as candy.
Mark the ⬭ to show your answer.

9. ⬭ say
⬭ silly
⬭ smile

10. ⬭ funny
⬭ fresh
⬭ fly

Home Activity This page practices words with the long *e* sound of *y*, as in *bumpy* and *sandy*. Work through the items with your child. Then challenge your child to choose three words he or she circled and use them in sentences.

Name_____

Read each story.
Circle the sentence that tells what the story is all about.
Then **circle** the picture that tells what the story is about.

1. Jill helps Mom.
   She picks up socks.
   She takes them to Mom.
   She sweeps up.

2.

3. Ben sees a cat.
   He sees a puppy.
   Then he sees a fish.
   Ben can see the pets.

4.

Read the story. **Write** a title for this story.

_____

5. _____

   Holly has fun at camp.
   She can go on hikes.
   She can swim in a lake.
   She can sleep in a tent too.

© Pearson Education A

School + Home

Home Activity This page helps your child identify main ideas of stories. Work through the items with your child. Then ask your child to make up titles for the first two little stories on this page.

94 **Comprehension Main Idea**   **Practice Book Unit 4**

Name_____

Circle a word to finish each sentence.
Write it on the line.

them   their

_____

- - - - - - - - - - - - - - - - - -

1. Ned and Pam see _____ dad.

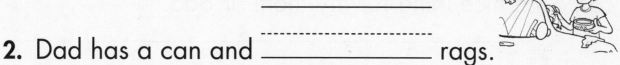

how   some

_____

- - - - - - - - - - - - - - - - - -

2. Dad has a can and _____ rags.

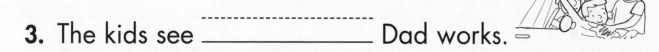

how   have

_____

- - - - - - - - - - - - - - - - - -

3. The kids see _____ Dad works.

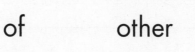

of   other

_____

- - - - - - - - - - - - - - - - - -

4. The kids pick up the _____ rags.

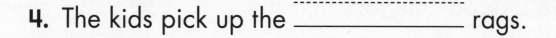

their   how

_____

- - - - - - - - - - - - - - - - - -

5. Ned and Pam help _____ dad.

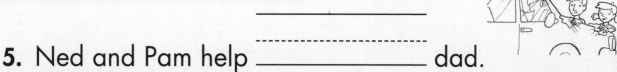

© Pearson Education A

School + Home   **Home Activity** This page helps your child learn to read and write the words *how, other, some,* and *their.* Write *How do you help at home?* on a sheet of paper. Help your child read the question aloud and surite an answer in a sentence.

Name_____

Finish the sentences. **Write** the words on the lines.
The words in the box may help you.

do well at school	help them
get a gift make my bed	go on a trip

I can do a nice thing for my mom or dad.

_____
1. I can _____ .

_____
2. I can _____ .

_____
3. I can _____ .

I can have a good time too!

_____
4. I can _____ .

_____
5. I can _____ .

Home Activity This page gives practice in finishing sentences. Help your child write the sentences. Then read them together. Ask your child to describe a surprise that he or she has given or received.

96 Writing   **Practice Book Unit 4**

© Pearson Education A

Name_____

Circle the word for each picture.

king

sink

1. 	2.	3.	4. 
bank bent	sing swing	truck tank	skunk skate

5. 	6. 	7. 	8. 
rink ring	bunk band	wind wing	sing slip

Find the word that has the same ending sound as .
Mark the ⬭ to show your answer.

9. ⬭ pink
⬭ pick
⬭ pile

10. ⬭ gum
⬭ jacks
⬭ junk

Home Activity This page practices words that end with *ng* and *nk*. Work through the items with your child. Then ask your child to make a list of words that rhyme with *wink, sank,* and *thing.*

Name_____

Say the word for each picture.
Write nk on the line if the word has the same ending sound as **pink**.
Write ng on the line if the word has the same ending sound as **sting**.

pi**nk**

sti**ng**

1.

sti _____

2.

sku _____

3.

spri _____

4.

ta _____

5.

ca _____

6.

stri _____

7.

ni _____

8.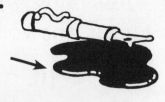

i _____

9.

wi _____

Home Activity This page practices words that end with *ing, ink, ank,* and *unk.* Work through the items with your child. Then have your child write the following words and use each in a sentence: *think, thank, junk,* and *bring.*

© Pearson Education A

Name_____

Read the story.
Circle the sentence that tells what the story is all about.
Then **circle** the picture that shows what the story is all about.

1. Jane looks happy.
She makes a glad face.
She smiles.
She grins.

3. Teddy walks the dog.
Teddy likes his dog.
He pets the dog.
Teddy hugs the dog.

5. Shan cut some shapes.
She stuck them on the shade.
She put on some dots.
Shan made a lamp look nice.

© Pearson Education A

 Home Activity This page helps your child identify the main idea in a story. Work through the items with your child. Then read one of your child's favorite stories. Ask him or her to tell you what the story is all about.

Name_____

Pick a word from the box to finish each sentence.
Write it on the line.

| any | friend | new | our |

1. This is _____ cat Skip.

2. We will make Skip a _____ home.

3. My _____ Kate is here too.

4. We don't need _____ help at all.

5. Skip has made a new _____ !

Home Activity This page helps your child learn to read and write the words *any, friend, new,* and *our.* Work through the items with your child. Help your child write these words on cards and practice reading them aloud.

100 **High-Frequency Words**   **Practice Book Unit 4**

© Pearson Education A

Name_____

Think of things you can make. **Finish** each sentence.
Write the words on the lines.
The words in each box may help you.

red	blue	green
yellow	happy	sad

1. Some kids make masks.

_____
- -
A mask can be _____ .

a dress	a hat
pants	a top

2. Some kids can make a doll.

_____
- -
A doll can have _____ .

Write a sentence that tells about a thing you can make.

_____
- -
3. _____

_____
- -
_____

Home Activity This page helps your child finish sentences and learn to write a sentence. Your child can use words from the boxes or other words. Help your child finish the sentences. Then talk about how the things can be made, or help your child make or draw the thing he or she wrote about in the last sentence.

Name_____

Pick a word from the box to finish
each compound word.
Write it on the line.
Draw a line to the picture it matches.

pancake

┌─────────────────────────────┐
│ **ball   box   cake   pack** │
└─────────────────────────────┘

1. base _____

2. cup _____

3. back _____

4. sand _____

5.

6.

7.

8.

Find the compound word.
Mark the ⬭ to show your answer.

9. ⬭ bedtime   10. ⬭ in
   ⬭ picnic   ⬭ inside
   ⬭ kitten   ⬭ sides

Home Activity This page provides practice recognizing compound words. Work through the items with
your child. Then help your child find things with names that are compound words, such as: *toothbrush,*
bathtub, and *flashlight.*

© Pearson Education A

Name_____

Say the word for each picture.
Write es if the picture shows
more than one.

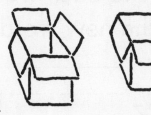

box**es**

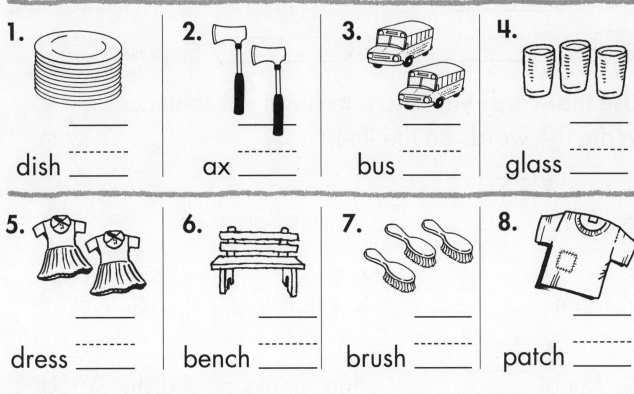

1.
dish _____

2.
ax _____

3.
bus _____

4.
glass _____

5.
dress _____

6.
bench _____

7.
brush _____

8.
patch _____

Pick a word from the box to finish each sentence.
Write it on the line.

inches	foxes

9. I saw two cute _____ .

10. One of them was 20 _____ long.

Home Activity This page helps your child add -es to nouns to make them mean more than one. Work through the items with your child. Then have your child choose three of the words with -es at the end and use them in one sentence.

Name_____

Add -es to each word.
Write the new word on the line.

1. buzz _____

2. munch _____

3. rush _____

4. mix _____

5. pass _____

Use the words you wrote to finish the sentences.
Write the words on the lines.

6. A bee _____ , and Sam runs.

7. Sam _____ to see Ming.

8. Ming _____ fun snacks on a dish.

9. Ming _____ the dish to Sam.

10. Sam _____ one of the snacks.

Home Activity This page helps your child practice adding -es to verbs. Work through the items with your child. Then have your child add -es to the following verbs and act out the actions: *mix, wax,* and *catch.*

Practice Book Unit 4

Name_____

Read the story.
Circle the sentence that tells what the story is all about.
Then **write** a title for the story.

---

1. Tess has one dog.
She has two cats.
She has three fish.
Tess has lots of pets.

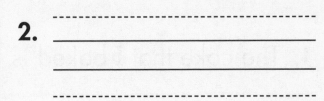

2. _____

---

3. Ruff likes to rest.
He sits in the hall.
Ruff sleeps on the rug.
He rests on the grass.

4. _____

---

5. We will go on a trip.
We will pack.
We will take a cab.
We will go on a plane.

6. _____

© Pearson Education A

School + Home

Home Activity This page helps your child identify the main idea of a story. Work through the items with your child. Then look at the stories together again. Ask your child to tell about each stroy in his or her own words.

Practice Book Unit 4

Comprehension Main Idea 105

Name_____

Pick a word from the box to finish each sentence.
Write it on the line.

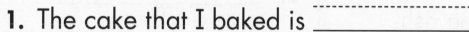

| again done know were |

1. The cake that I baked is _____ .

2. We _____ that it is big.

3. My last two cakes _____ not this big.

4. Now will you make a cake _____ ?

5. We like it when a cake is _____ .

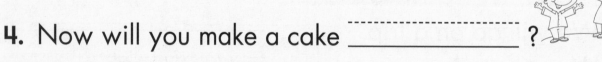

© Pearson Education A

Home Activity This page helps your child learn to read and write the words *again, done, know,* and *were.* Work through the items with your child. Say the words one at a time. Ask your child to use each word in a sentence.

Name_____

Think of a story, or tale, with someone who hunts for treasure. **Read** each question. **Write** your answer on the line. The words in the box may help you.

a gem	**a ring that shines**	**in a bag**	**by a tree**
in a box	**a fancy stone**	**in a hole**	

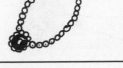

1. Who will hunt for good things?

_____

_____ will hunt.

2. What things can be in the tale?

_____

The things can be _____ .

3. Where can the things be?

_____

The things can be _____ .

4. What can be done to get the things?

_____

_____

Home Activity This page gives practice in writing sentences to plan a story. Help your child write the sentences. Read the sentences together. Then have your child draw a picture to show one event from his or her story.

© Pearson Education A

Name_____

f**or**k    st**ore**

Say the word for each picture. Circle the word.

1.    corn
cone

2.   storm
stone

3.    port
pot

4.    code
core

5.    home
horn

6.    thorn
toss

7. 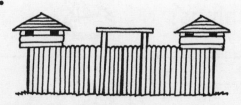   fort
fog

8.    stock
stork

Home Activity This page practices words with the sound of *or* heard in *fork* and *ore* heard in *store*. Name each picture. Then say these words to your child: *sore, tack, cord, car, porch, star, mark, more.* Have your child stand if a word has an *or/ore* sound and sit if it does not.

Name_____

Say the word for each picture.
Circle the word.

f**ar**m

1.

car
core
cot

2.

jot
jab
jar

3.

yam
yak
yarn

4.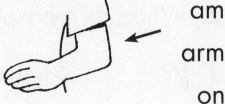

am
arm
on

5.

pan
park
port

6.

cab
card
cord

7.

star
stack
store

8.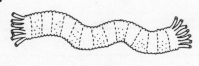

score
scope
scarf

9.

cord
cast
cart

10.

shark
short
shake

© Pearson Education A

School + Home

Home Activity This page practices words with the *ar* sound heard in *farm*. Name each picture and work through the items with your child. Then have your child tell you a short story about a visit to a farm. Encourage your child to use at least three words that have the *ar* sound.

Name_____

Look at the picture. **Circle** the answer to each question. **Hint:** One question will have two answers.

Dad   Meg

1. Who has a rag?   Meg   Dad

2. Who has a hose?   Meg   Dad

3. Who has glasses?   Meg   Dad

4. Who has pants?   Meg   Dad

5. Who has a top with dots?   Meg   Dad

6. Write one other way that Meg and her dad are the same.

_____
- -
_____

7. Write one other way that Meg and her dad are NOT the same.

_____
- -
_____

© Pearson Education A

School +Home **Home Activity** This page helps your child identify how two people are alike and different. Work through the items with your child. Then ask your child to name one way the two of you are alike and one way the two of you are different.

Name_____

Pick a word from the box to finish each sentence.
Write it on the line.

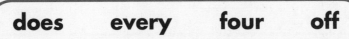

does   every   four   off

1. Rick _____ chores at home.

2. He sweeps the porch _____ day.

3. He uses a rag to wipe _____ marks.

4. There are _____ fish to feed, too.

5. Rick _____ a lot to help at home.

Home Activity This page helps your child learn to read and write the words *does, every, four,* and *off.* Write each word on a card and lay the cards facedown. Have your child pick up each card, say the word, and use it in a sentence.

© Pearson Education A

Name_____

Think about a special time in your life. **Read** the questions. **Finish** the sentences. The words in the box may help you.

friends	at a park	had a party	ate good things
Dad	played games	at home	went for a ride

1. Who were you with?

   _____

   I was with _____ .

2. Where were you?

   _____

   I was _____ .

3. What did you do?

   _____

   I _____ .

4. **Draw** a picture about the fun time you had.

5. **Write** a sentence about your picture.

   _____

   _____

   _____

© Pearson Education A

Name_____

h**er**   b**ir**d   c**ur**l

Say the word for each picture. **Circle** the word.

1.		skirt skit	2.	 girl get
3.		burn barn	4.	 fin fern
5.		dart dirt	6.	porch perch
7.		shirt sharp	8.	 cluck clerk

Find the word that has the same middle sound as .

Mark the ⬭ to show your answer.

9. ⬭ firm
   ⬭ form
   ⬭ farm

10. ⬭ tune
    ⬭ torn
    ⬭ turn

 Home Activity This page practices words spelled with *er, ir,* and *ur* with the sound heard in the middle of *her, dirt,* and *turn.* Make up riddles about the pictures, such as: *I am green and I grow. What am I?* (fern) Have your child point to the correct picture and say its name.

© Pearson Education A

Name_____

Double the last letter in each word. **Add -ed** to each word. **Write** the new word on the line.

1. rip _____   **2.** drop _____

Double the last letter in each word. **Add -ing** to each word. **Write** the new word on the line.

3. shop _____   **4.** grab _____

Use the words you wrote to finish the sentences. **Write** the words on the lines.

5. Mom and Sam are _____ .

6. Sam is _____ a bag for Mom.

7. Sam _____ the bag.

8. The bag _____ and made a mess.

Home Activity This page practices writing words that end in -ed and -ing, such as planned and stopping. Write the following words on a sheet of paper and have your child add -ed and -ing to each one: clap, nod, hum. Have your child act out each word.

114 **Phonics** Endings -ed, -ing Double Final Consonant   **Practice Book Unit 4**

Name_____

Look at the pictures. **Write** to tell about the pets. **Use** the words in the box. **Hint:** You will use one set of words two times.

bird   fish

has fins	has wings	in a tank	in a cage
must eat	has feet	can swim	

bird   fish

1. _____   5. _____

2. _____   6. _____

3. _____   7. _____

4. _____   8. _____

Home Activity This page helps your child identify how two animals are alike and different. Help your child name another way birds and fish are alike and different, such as: *Birds and fish have tails. Birds can fly but fish cannot fly.*

Practice Book Unit 4   **Comprehension** Compare and Contrast   **115**

Name_____

Pick a word from the box to finish each sentence.
Write it on the line.

about family once together

1. My _____ likes to ride bikes.

2. We ride our bikes _____ a week.

3. We sit _____ and rest.

4. It is _____ time to go.

5. It is fun to ride with my _____ !

© Pearson Education A

Home Activity This page helps your child learn to read and write the words *about*, *family*, *once*, and *together*. Point to the words in the box one at a time. Have your child say each word aloud and use it in a sentence.

Name_____

Think about something you have that you like a lot.
Draw a picture of it in the box. **Read** the questions.
Finish the sentences on the lines.

1. [ ]

2. What is it?

_____

It is _____ .

3. What does it look like?

_____

It is _____ .

4. Where did you get it?

_____

I got it _____ .

5. What do you do with it?

_____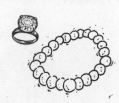

I _____ .

Home Activity This page helps your child practice writing sentences to describe a special object he or she owns. Work with your child to write the sentences. Then read them together. If possible, let your child hold the object while reading.

Name_____

Write the contraction for each
pair of words.   **He is** tired.
                      He's tired.

_____
1. she + is = -----------------
              _____

              _____
2. it + is =   -----------------
              _____

              _____
3. here + is = -----------------
              _____

              _____
4. who + is = -----------------
              _____

              _____
5. that + is = -----------------
              _____

              _____
6. what + is = -----------------
              _____

Find the contraction.
Mark the ⬭ to show your answer.

7. ⬭ whats   8. ⬭ that's
   ⬭ he's   ⬭ this
   ⬭ there   ⬭ hats

© Pearson Education A

Home Activity This page practices making contractions with 's, such as *here's*. Work through the items with your child. Then ask your child to use the words *he's, she's,* and *it's* in sentences.

118 **Phonics Contraction** *'s*   **Practice Book Unit 4**

Name_____

Pick a word from the box that means the same as each pair of words. **Write** it on the line.

you're	they've	I've
you've	they're	we've

We are pals.
We're pals.

1. we + have =

_____
- - - - - - - - - - -
_____

2. you + are =

_____
- - - - - - - - - - -
_____

3. I + have =

_____
- - - - - - - - - - -
_____

4. you + have =

_____
- - - - - - - - - - -
_____

Look at each picture. **Write** the contraction to finish each sentence.

They're	I've	They've

5. _____ in a box.

6. _____ won a prize.

Home Activity This page practices making contractions with 've and 're, such as we've and they're. Work through the items with your child. Then write we, they, he, she, is, are, and have on index cards and see how many contractions your child can make.

© Pearson Education A

Name_____

Read the sentences in the story.
Write 1, 2, 3 to show the right order.

1. _____ Kim shares her grapes
with Lan.

2. _____ Kim has some grapes.

3. _____ Lan wants some grapes too.

Read the sentence that begins the story. **Write** a
sentence that could be in the middle of the story.
Write a sentence that could end the story.

Jack has a ball.

4. _____

_____

5. _____

Home Activity This page helps your child identify the beginning, middle, and end of a story. Work through
the items with your child. Then ask your child to tell you different things he or she did today in the order that
they happened.

Name_____

Pick a word from the box to finish each sentence.
Write it on the line.

give   great   many   people

1. Max and Ann are kind _____ .

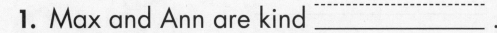

2. They _____ books to kids.

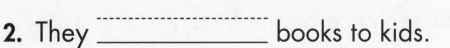

3. Ann is _____ at helping with pets.

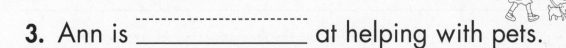

4. Max likes to _____ food from his garden.

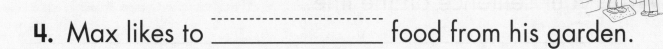

5. Max and Ann have _____ friends.

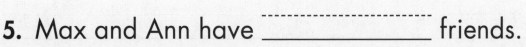

Home Activity This page helps your child learn to read and write the words *give*, *great*, *many*, and *people*.
Work through the items with your child. Help your child think of ways he or she can help around the house or
in the neighborhood.

© Pearson Education A

Name_____

Finish each sentence.
Write the words on the lines.

_____
1. I can share _____ .

_____
2. I can give _____ .

Write a sentence telling what you can share with a
friend. **Write** your sentence on the line.

_____
3. _____
_____

Write a sentence telling how you can help at home.
Write your sentence on the line.

_____
4. _____
_____

© Pearson Education A

Home Activity This page helps your child finish sentences and learn to write sentences. Help your child
write the sentences. Then together, talk about other ways he or she can share with a friend or neighbor.

Name_____

Circle the word for each picture.

tall   tall**er**   tall**est**

1.

faster   fastest

2.

hotter   hot

3.

bigger   biggest

4.

thicker   thickest

5.

sadder   saddest

6.

thinner   thinnest

Write **er** or **est** to finish the word in each sentence.

Rose   Lucy

7. Lucy has long _____ hair.

8. The little dog has the long _____ tail.

Home Activity This page practices words ending with -er and -est that compare things. Work through the items with your child. Then look through magazines or catalogs together. Have your child compare people or objects using words with the -er or -est ending.

Name_____

Pick a word from the box to finish each sentence.
Write it on the line.

> bridge   budge   hedge   fudge   ledge

1. Max is under the _____ .

2. Puff is on the _____ .

3. Chip is behind the _____ .

4. Our friends just won't _____ .

5. Let's give them some _____ !

School + Home **Home Activity** This page practices words that end with *dge* that have the sound heard in *badge*. Work through the items with your child. Then have your child write the *dge* words from this page on a piece of paper. Work together to think of other words to add to the list.

Name_____

Read each story. **Look** at the pictures.
Write 1, 2, 3 to show the right order.

Brent had a bike.
Brent rode too fast.
Brent hit a bump and fell.
Dad helped him to get up.

1. ☐  **2.** ☐  **3.** ☐

Min planted seeds.
She put them in the sun.
She gave them water.
The plants got bigger and bigger.

4. ☐  **5.** ☐  **6.** ☐

© Pearson Education A

 School + Home **Home Activity** This page helps your child learn about the order in which events happen in a story. Work through the items with your child. Have your child tell you what he or she does to get ready for school in the morning. Ask what is done first, second, and third.

Practice Book Unit 5   **Comprehension** Sequence **125**

Name_____

Pick a word from the box to finish each sentence.
Write it on the line.

| away   find   long   took |

1. Ana _____ her dog Tag to the park.

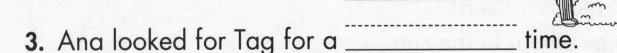

2. Tag ran _____ when he saw a cat.

3. Ana looked for Tag for a _____ time.

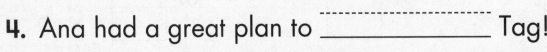

4. Ana had a great plan to _____ Tag!

5. She called for Tag like a cat.

It didn't take _____ for Tag to come running!

© Pearson Education A

Name_____

Think of a problem you had.
How did you solve the problem?
Write the steps in the chart.

Problem

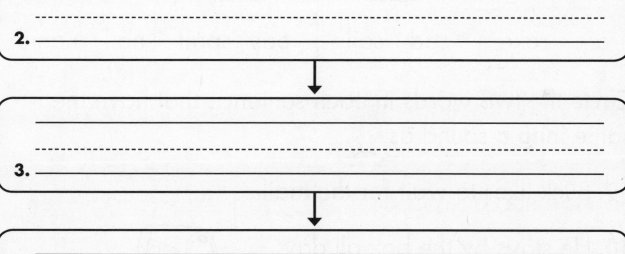

Steps I Took

1.

2.

3.

4.

Home Activity This page helps your child learn to write sentences that tell what happened in order. Help your child write the sentences. Cut apart the boxes with the sentences. Then mix up the sentences and have your child put them in the correct order.

© Pearson Education A

Name_____

Say the word for each picture.
Circle the word.

tr**ai**n    h**ay**

1. 	**2.**	**3.** 	**4.** 
paint park	smell snail	paid play	trip tray
5. 	**6.** 	**7.** 	**8.**
rain rake	sad sail	pay pail	nail name

Circle the two words in each sentence that have the same **long a** sound as .

9. Buck likes to wait for the mail.

10. He stays by the box all day.

Home Activity This page practices words with the long a sound spelled *ay* and *ai* heard in *stay* and *brain*. Work through the items with your child. Then have your child use the words from this page in a silly rhyme.

© Pearson Education A

Name_____

Say the word for each picture.
Circle the word.

m<u>ea</u>t

1.

beans   bell

2.

sell   seal

3.

jelly   jeans

4.

steam   sick

5.

tale   team

6.

meal   miss

7.

peach   pat

8.

class   clean

Find the word that has the same **long e** sound as .
Mark the ⊂⊃ to show your answer.

9. ⊂⊃ beak
    ⊂⊃ back
    ⊂⊃ best

10. ⊂⊃ tell
    ⊂⊃ trap
    ⊂⊃ teach

© Pearson Education A

 Home Activity This page practices words with the long e sound spelled ea heard in *dream*. Work through the items with your child. Then have your child use each word in a sentence.

Name _____

Look at the pictures.
Write 1, 2, 3 to put the sentences in order.

1. Kate put ice cream in the glass. _____

2. Kate ate her treat. _____

3. She added some nuts. _____

4. Then Ed trained Sam to beg. _____

5. Ed trained his dog Sam to sit. _____

6. Ed gave Sam treats after his tricks. _____

Home Activity This page helps your child put events in order to form a story. Work through the items with your child. Ask your child to draw a series of pictures showing three events in the order in which they happened.

Name_____

Pick a word to finish each sentence.
Write it on the line.

don't   most   won't   write

_____

1. When it is cold, _____ kids stay inside.

_____

2. We _____ know what to do.

_____

3. We can _____ a story.

4. We can bake a cake.

_____

We _____ make a mess!

_____

5. We can play _____ games.

We can play hide and seek!

Home Activity This page helps your child learn to read and write the words *don't, most, won't,* and *write.* Work through the items with your child. Talk with your child about all the things he or she can do in the house on a rainy or snowy day.

Practice Book Unit 5

High-Frequency Words **131**

© Pearson Education A

Name_____

Finish each sentence. Write the words on the lines.

1. What can I do?

_____

I can write a _____ .

2. What can I do?

_____

I can make a _____ .

_____

3. What can I do? I can find a _____ .

4. What can I do for my friends?

_____

_____

_____

5. What can I do for my family?

_____

_____

_____

School + Home **Home Activity** This page helps your child learn to write sentences. Work with your child to write each sentence. Then together think of new ways your family can help each other. Try to think of one idea for each day of the week.

Name_____

Add **'s** or **'** to the end of each word.

cat**s'** dish    Kim**'s** cat

---

1. Chad _____ pet

2. girls _____ kites

---

3. man _____ hat

4. dogs _____ ball

---

5. jars _____ lids

6. Brit _____ dress

Pick a word from the box to match each picture.
Write it on the line.

(**baby's   birds'**)

7. _____ nests

8. _____ blocks

Home Activity This page practices words that show ownership. Work through the items with your child. Then walk around the house with your child, pointing out objects owned by one or more family members. Ask your child to use a word to tell you who owns each object, such as *Jen's lamp* or *the boys' bedroom*.

Name_____

Say the word for each picture. Circle the word.
Write it on the line.

m<u>ow</u>   s<u>oa</u>p

1.
bone
bow
be

_____

2.
coat
cot
code

_____

3.
bat
back
boat

_____

4.
snow
sap
stop

_____

5.
gap
got
goat

_____

© Pearson Education A

Home Activity This page practices words with the long o sound spelled *oa* and *ow* heard in *toad* and *row*. Help your child write the long o words on this page on index cards. Ask him or her to sort the cards by their spellings.

Name_____

Look at both pictures. **Write** sentences to tell how the pictures are the same and different.

Same

Ray

1. _____
_ _ _ _ _ _ _ _ _ _ _ _ _ _ _

2. _____
_ _ _ _ _ _ _ _ _ _ _ _ _ _ _

3. _____

Different

Jay

1. _____
_ _ _ _ _ _ _ _ _ _ _ _ _ _ _

2. _____
_ _ _ _ _ _ _ _ _ _ _ _ _ _ _

3. _____

© Pearson Education A

Home Activity This page helps your child write about how two things are the same and different. Work through the items with your child. Then ask your child to point out all the ways the two of you are the same and different.

Name_____

Read the sentence. **Unscramble** the letters. **Use** the words in the box. **Write** the word on the line.

over   push   should   would

1. I **ouwld** like some help.

_____
- - - - - - - - - - - - -
_____

2. Put the word *dog* **vroe** that line.

_____
- - - - - - - - - - - - -
_____

3. Now **shpu** "enter."

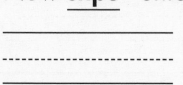

_____
- - - - - - - - - - - - -
_____

4. You **holsud** look in this too.

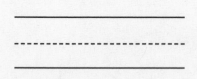

_____
- - - - - - - - - - - - -
_____

© Pearson Education A

Home Activity This page helps your child learn to read and write the words *over*, *push*, *should*, and *would*. Work through the items with your child. Then have your child use each word in a sentence.

Name_____

Look at the chart. Write words on the lines.
Keep your list.

When I Need to Find an Answer

Where I Can Look	Who I Can Ask	What I Can Do
1. _____	4. _____	7. _____
2. _____	5. _____	8. _____
3. _____	6. _____	9. _____

Home Activity This page helps your child write a list of ways he or she can find answers to questions. Help your child fill in the chart. Then have your child tell you one question for which he or she wants an answer. Use the list to help your child find the answer.

© Pearson Education A

Name_____

Change y to i.
Add -es and -ed to each word.
Write the new words on the lines.

cr**ies**   cr**ied**

	Add -es	Add -ed
1. try		
2. spy		
3. dry		
4. fry		

Change y to i. Add -er and -est to each word.
Write the new words on the lines.

	Add -er	Add -est
5. funny		
6. lucky		

Home Activity This page practices adding endings to words in which the spelling changes from *y* to *i*. Work through the items with your child. Have your child add *-ed* to the words *hurry* and *study* and then use the new words in sentences.

© Pearson Education A

Name_____

Say the word for each picture. **Pick** letters from the box to finish each word. **Write** the letters on the lines.

<u>str</u>eam

| scr | shr | spl | str | thr |

1. _____ ee

2. _____ ash

3. _____ ing

4. _____ een

5. _____ ub

6. _____ one

7. _____ eet

8. _____ imp

9. _____ ow

10. _____ ipe

© Pearson Education A

Home Activity This page practices words that begin with three-letter blends. Work through the items with your child. Then have your child name each picture and use each word in a sentence.

Name_____

Read each story. **Find** the sentence that tells what the story is about. **Circle** that sentence. **Write** a title that tells what the story is about.

1. Danny likes the park.
   He likes to ride his bike there.
   He likes to play on the grass.
   He can fly a kite at the park too.

   _____

2. _____

3. Fran got a big sheet.
   She got some yarn and tape.
   She got some pens.
   Fran made a funny mask.

   _____

4. _____

5. Sho cannot go to school.
   Sho is sick today.
   He will stay in bed.
   Sho will get lots of rest.

   _____

6. _____

Home Activity This page helps your child identify the main idea of a story. Work through the items with your child. Then have your child use his or her own words to tell you what each story is about.

© Pearson Education A

Name_____

Pick a word from the box to finish each sentence.
Write it on the line.

behind   love   pull   soon

1. Min and Carl _____ to make things.

2. Min made a box to _____ her bunny.

3. Carl made a box to _____ his dog.

4. Min and Carl put the boxes _____ them.

5. They _____ go for a walk.

 Home Activity This page helps your child learn to read and write the words *behind, love, pull,* and *soon.* Have your child make up a sentence using each of the words.

© Pearson Education A

Name_____

Think of something that can make life easier. **Draw** a picture of it in the box. **Write** about it on the lines.

1.

2. What will you call it?

_____

- -

_____

3. What can it do?

_____

- -

_____

4. Who will it help?

_____

- -

_____

5. How will it make life easier?

_____

- -

_____

© Pearson Education A

School + Home

Home Activity This page practices writing sentences about an invention. Help your child write the sentences and read them. Then have your child look around your home for three inventions that make life easier.

Name_____

Circle a word to finish each sentence.
Write it on the line.

tie

light

nine night
_____

1. It gets dark at _____ .

lie like
_____

2. We _____ in our tent.

pay pie
_____

3. We eat some _____ .

his high
_____

4. We look up _____ .

bright bring
_____

5. The stars are _____ .

Home Activity This page practices words with the long *i* sound spelled *ie* and *igh* heard in *die* and *sight*. Work through the items with your child. Have your child look at the page and find long *i* words that rhyme. (*light/night/bright* and *tie/lie/pie/high*)

Practice Book Unit 5   **Phonics Long *i*: *ie*, *igh* 143**

© Pearson Education A

Name_____

Say the word for each picture.
Circle the word.

cand<u>le</u>

1.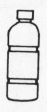

bottle

bone

2.

turned

turtle

3.

needle

needing

4.

table

tab

5.

adding

apple

6.

pickle

picked

Pickles

7.

pump

puddle

8.

buddy

bubble

Find the word that has the same ending sound as .
Mark the ⬭ to show your answer.

9. ⬭ ride
   ⬭ riddle
   ⬭ ring

10. ⬭ hang
    ⬭ handy
    ⬭ handle

 Home Activity This page practices reading two-syllable words that end with *le*. Name each picture and work through the items with your child. Then write *little, middle, rattle,* and *tattle* and help your child read the words.

© Pearson Education A

Name_____

Read the story.

Do you need to go on a trip? You can go in many ways. You can go by car. You can go on a ship. You can go on a train or plane.

---

1. **Circle** the big idea of the story.

   It is fun to go on a trip.

   You can go places in many ways.

2. **Circle** the best title for the story.

   Many Ways to Go

   A Long Trip

---

3. **Draw** a picture in the box to show the big idea.

4. **Write** a sentence that tells about your picture.

© Pearson Education A

Home Activity This page helps your child identify the main idea of a story. Work through the items with your child. Then ask your child to tell you how he or she would like to travel and why.

Practice Book Unit 5　　　　　　**Comprehension Main Idea** **145**

Name_____

Pick a word from the box to finish each sentence.
Write it on the line.

| before   kind   none   sure |

1. What _____ of car is that?

2. We have not seen it _____ .

3. There are _____ like that on our street.

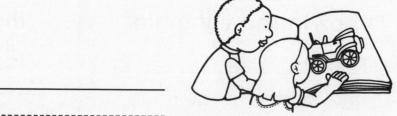

4. Here is the same _____ of car.

5. It _____ looks fun to ride in!

© Pearson Education A

Home Activity This page helps your child learn to read and write the words *before, kind, none,* and *sure.*
Work through the items together. Then have your child use these words to describe a fun car to ride in.

Name_____

Think about the way people did chores long ago.
Think about the way people do chores now.
Write your ideas on the lines.

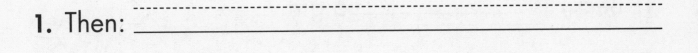

Clean dirty socks and shirts

_____

1. Then: _____

_____

2. Now: _____

Make meals

_____

3. Then: _____

_____

4. Now: _____

Go to the store

_____

5. Then: _____

_____

6. Now: _____

Home Activity This page practices writing sentences. Help your child write the sentences and then read them together. Ask your child to tell whether it is harder or easier to do chores now. Have your child explain his or her answer.

Name_____

Drop the final **e.**
Add -ed or **-ing** to the word in ( ).
Write the new word on the line.

(make + ing)

_____

1. Becky is _____ a gift.

(wipe + ed)

_____

2. She _____ the can with a rag.

(glue + ed)

_____

3. She _____ stars on the can.

(hope + ing)

_____

4. Becky is _____ that Dad will come soon.

(smile + ed)

_____

5. Dad took the gift and _____ .

Home Activity This page practices adding *-ed* and *-ing* to words that end in e. Work through the items with your child. Then write *bake* and *hike* on a sheet of paper. Have your child add *-ed* and *-ing* to each one and write the new words.

© Pearson Education A

Name_____

Say the word for each picture. **Circle** the word.

p**ony**

1.

wags wagon

2.

tiger   tile

3.

some   sofa

4.

ripped river

5.

cabin camp

6.

spider   spill

7.

robot   robe

8.

came camel

Pick a word from the box to match each picture.
Write it on the line.

lemon   baby

9.

_____

10.

_____

School + Home   **Home Activity** This page practices two-syllable words that have one consonant in the middle. Name each picture. Work through the items with your child. Then have your child choose three words and use each one in a sentence.

Name_____

Read the story.

Tony looks in the mailbox. He sees a box.
The box has his name on it! Tony opens the
box. A car is inside. It is a gift from his uncle.

1. **Circle** the big idea of
   the story.

   Tony gets a gift.
   Tony sees a box.

2. **Circle** the best title for
   the story.

   A Funny Box
   Tony's Gift

Read the story.

Tony makes a ramp. He puts his car on
top. Then he lets go. The car runs down
the ramp. It is very fast! Tony plays
again and again. His new car is a lot of fun!

3. **Circle** the big idea of
   the story.

   Tony likes to make ramps.
   Tony has fun with his car.

4. **Circle** the best title for
   the story.

   A Fun Car
   Time to Drive

5. **Write** a sentence telling what the two stories are about.

_____
- -
_____

_____
- -
_____

© Pearson Education A

Home Activity This page helps your child identify the main idea of a story. Work through the items with your child. Then have your child imagine that the two stories come from one book. Ask your child to make up a title for the book.

Name_____

Pick a word from the box to finish each sentence.
Write it on the line.

| because   goes   live   school |

_____

1. I _____ with my family

_____

2. Dad takes me to _____ each day.

_____

3. I like my art class _____ it is fun.

_____

4. I made a plane at _____ .

_____

5. My plane _____ up high!

© Pearson Education A

School + Home

Home Activity This page helps your child learn to read and write the words *because, goes, live,* and *school.* Write each word on an index card and place the cards facedown. Have your child pick up one card at a time and read each word.

Name_____

Think of new ways you can use things.
Write your ideas on the lines.

1. What can you do with a box?

_____
- -
_____

2. What can you do with a can?

_____
- -
_____

3. What can you do with a sock?

_____
- -
_____

4. Draw one of your
   ideas in the box.

5. Write a sentence about your picture.

_____
- -
_____
- -
_____

Home Activity This page practices writing sentences. Help your child write the sentences and read them together. Have your child choose one of the ideas on the page. Then have him or her tell you how to make the item.

Words I Can Now Read and Write

_____   _____
--------------------------   --------------------------
_____   _____

_____   _____
--------------------------   --------------------------
_____   _____

_____   _____
--------------------------   --------------------------
_____   _____

_____   _____
--------------------------   --------------------------
_____   _____

_____   _____
--------------------------   --------------------------
_____   _____

_____   _____
--------------------------   --------------------------
_____   _____

_____   _____
--------------------------   --------------------------
_____   _____

© Pearson Education A

Name_____

Words I Can Now Read and Write

- -

- -

- -

- -

- -

- -

- -

- -

Practice Book

Name_____

I read _____

_____

It was about

Words I Can Now Read and Write

_____   _____

_____   _____

Name_____

I read _____

_____

_____

It was about

Words I Can Now Read and Write

_____

_____